A CARTLOAD OF SCROLLS

A CARTLOAD OF SCROLLS

100 POEMS

IN THE MANNER OF

T'ANG DYNASTY POET

HAN-SHAN

JAMES P. LENFESTEY

HOLY COW! PRESS · DULUTH, MINNESOTA · 2007

Library of Congress Cataloging-in-Publication Data

Lenfestey, James P.
A cartload of scrolls : 100 poems in the manner of T'ang Dynasty poet Han-shan / by James P. Lenfestey.
    p. cm.
ISBN-13: 978-0-9779458-5-6 (alk. paper)
I. Title.
PS3612.E528C37 2007
811'.6—c22   2007015112

This project is supported in part by donations from generous individuals.

Holy Cow! Press books are distributed to the trade by Consortium Book Sales & Distribution, c/o Perseus Distribution, 1094 Flex Drive, Jackson, Tennessee 38301.

For personal inquiries, write to: Holy Cow! Press,
Post Office Box 3170, Mount Royal Station, Duluth, Minnesota 55803

Please visit our website: www.holycowpress.org

ACKNOWLEDGMENTS

Some of these poems first appeared or are forthcoming in the following publications, some in earlier versions. Many thanks to their editors for permission to reprint.

Askew, The Aurorean, Chronicle Alternative, Concrete Wolf, Free Verse, Lilliput Review, Mid-America Poetry Review, Nerve Cowboy, Northeast, Poetry East, Tundra, Urthona (UK).

Twenty-one poems first appeared in the collection, *Han-shan is the Cure for Warts,* published by Red Dragonfly Press, a letterpress edition of 200 standard copies, 26 deluxe, 2006.

"What Am I Doing Now That I'm in Paradise?" is reprinted from the chapbook *Saying Grace,* Marsh River Editions, 2005.

My gratitude to the Anderson Center, Red Wing, Minnesota for a residency to develop this manuscript, to Scott King for publishing the letterpress edition, *Han-shan is the Cure for Warts,* to poet Jay P. White, book artist Robert Johnson, quilter Chrissie Mahaffy and poetic videographer Mike Hazard for careful readings of the manuscript and many valuable suggestions, and to poet Thomas R. Smith, without whose talents as poet, reader, editor and friend, this manuscript would languish in a heap.

To Burton Watson,

whose musical translations

allowed me to hear Han-shan's songs.

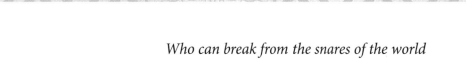

HANSHANNERS

by James P. Lenfestey

The story of my meeting the poetry of Han-shan and what it has come to mean to me is recorded in the following poems themselves. What should also be clear is that my great delight is not just in Han-shan's honest, sometimes antic, sometimes meditative sensibility, but the form in which he expresses it — the ancient lü-shih "regulated verse" lyric of Chinese poetry. In *Chinese Lyricism* (Columbia University Press, 1971), scholar and translator Burton Watson describes Chinese poetry's evolution from a four character line to a reenergized five or seven character line around 200 AD, and its preeminence for a thousand years thereafter. It reached its peak in the T'ang Dynasty (618-907), China's Elizabethan Age of poetry, with Li Bai, Du Fu, Wang Wei and a host of others, including Han-shan. The *lü-shih* is commonly translated into English in the eight line verse form of the original.

The subject matter is often mundane — listening to birds, missing one's family, wondering about friends, small or large regrets and joys, the search for meditative stillness. There is a combination of Taoist paradox, Buddhist clarity and ordinary angst — our lives are full of longings, but in the end we might as well try to quiet our monkey minds and still our appetites, or at least some of them, wine a useful exception.

As important, there is a clear rhetorical structure — an opening line or couplet that establishes the scene, followed by images that flesh it out in simple parallel sentences, and a final couplet that "takes us out" with a surprise or even a laugh.

Here's a Han-shan masterpiece of the form, as translated by Watson:

> *The birds in their chatter overwhelm me with feeling:*
> *At times like this I lie down in my straw hut.*
> *Cherries shine with crimson fire.*
> *Willows trail slender boughs.*
> *The morning sun pops from the jaws of blue peaks.*
> *Bright clouds are washed in the green pond.*
> *Who would have thought that I would leave the dusty world*
> *and come bounding up the southern slope of Cold Mountain?*
> — Watson, #39

I first encountered Han-shan's poems in 1970 through Gary Snyder's translations tucked in the back of *Riprap and Cold Mountain Poems*, a book enthusiastically shown to me by students in the first class I taught as a college English instructor. While living in Massachusetts in 1974 as director of an alternative high school, I discovered Watson's *Cold Mountain Poems: 100 Poems by the T'ang Poet Han-Shan* (Columbia University Press, 1970). Watson's Han-shan lyrics are colloquial, sometimes deeply thoughtful, at other times ironic or satiric, all with the rhythm of a mini-editorial and occasionally the punch line of a good joke. His Han-shan was the first poet to make me laugh out loud. Watson's book in hand, I began, for the first and only time in my life, to "write back" to an author, a "correspondence" I have kept up for more than thirty years.

Watson was an especially lucky hit among translators. As he explained in *Chinese Lyricism*, he faced many choices with classical characters in which nouns have no indication of number and verbs no indication of subject, tense or mood. His genius is to transform such inferences into poetic American English. Eliot Weinberger, in an illuminating essay on the profound impact of Asian poetry on American poetry in the early 20th century, calls Watson "unquestionably the greatest of all" postwar translators (*The New Directions Anthology of Classical Chinese Poetry*, New Directions, 2003). Watson revealed one reason why in a 2005 interview with *Translation Review*. In addition to seeking advice from poets such as Snyder and Cid Corman, "I have found that the best procedure is to read as much good contemporary poetry as possible, since contemporary American English is the idiom I wish to use in my poetry translations." In my own interview with Watson in Tokyo in 2006, I found him an exceptionally moving reader of poetry, deeply affected by both rhythm and mood. All of these qualities makes his translations sing to these American ears.

Then there is the character of Han-shan himself, who comes especially alive in Watson's collection because the poems are placed in chronological order based upon internal evidence, and Watson selected only the poems rich in human content.

No one knows Han-shan's real name — he took the name "Cold Mountain" from the place in the T'ien-t'ai Mountains where he lived his last years. No one knows exactly where he came from. From evidence in his poems, we know he once lived in a city, rode a white horse, had a wife and son. We do not know why the family separated — banishment, war, personal failure, his wife's death are all possibilities — or how he became poor. He was certainly raised a member of the educated class and, like most, banged his head more than once against the civil service examination system that served as the gateway to a significant job. Now "retired," he lives a hermit's life, needing little, wanting nothing, accepting occasional handouts from his pal Shih-te working in the kitchen of the nearby Kuo-ch'ing temple while visiting his friend, the monk Feng-kan. Bill Porter, AKA Red Pine, the American Buddhist translator of *The Collected Songs of Cold Mountain* (Copper Canyon Press, ©2000) and an expert in Chinese Buddhism and culture, believes Han-shan probably lived at the temple during the winter, easily slipping in among the thousand or so monks. Probably a lay Buddhist, Han-shan readily admits his struggles to still his mind. Nor has he forgotten how to laugh uproariously at his own youthful passions and despair, the pomposity of stuffed-shirt scholars, and high officials who bow down to him as an incarnated Buddha-on-earth.

Finally, while many of Han-shan's nearly 300 poems include conventional Buddhist exhortations and laments, some reflect a private tension common in Chinese poetry and painting between Confucian devotion to family, community and service in the urban world of "red dust," and a monkish longing for simple labor and peaceful contemplation among landscapes of "mountains and rivers without end."

In the end, Han-shan resolved that debate into a hermit's life. Were his poems not gathered from rocks and trees and temple walls into a collection by an admiring public official (or so the legend goes), his voice would have vanished without a trace, as have those of tens of thousands of poets before and since, as he himself is said to have vanished, laughing wildly, into a crack in the face of a cliff which closed up behind him.

Han-shan left behind an open, antic, outsider sensibility easy for Americans to love. This puzzles the Chinese, who rarely study his poems today, although youthful portraits of him with long time pal Shih-te remain symbols of lasting friendship and even-oddly-long marriage.

What remains open to all is the sturdy poetic container that T'ang poets like Han-shan employed, approximations available to us through Watson's, Snyder's and Red Pine's translations among many others, into which one can pour similar mundane longings, wonderings and ravings. The eight line length and rhetorical structure offer enough room for readers to enter, roll around for a while, then slip back out.

Few of the poems in this collection strictly follow the translated *lü-shih* form — some are nine lines, others seven or even five or four. Most vary in other ways. But all, I hope, contain a certain sensibility — one that seems to fit my own voice as well as that of my "older brother" Han-shan.

Knowing of my more than thirty-year practice with this form, the gifted young poet Thor Bacon dubbed these modern versions "Hanshanners." Works for me, and I hope for you.

Minneapolis
Winter Solstice, 2006

NOTE: When any of the following poems involved a response to a particular poem of Han-Shan's as translated by Burton Watson, I have included the poem's number from *Cold Mountain Poems: 100 Poems by the Tang Poet Han-Shan.*

TABLE OF CONTENTS

1

FINDING MY OLDER BROTHER

In history this never happens.

But in life, all the time.

My older brother, who died before he was born,

has been found!

He is 1,200 years old, more or less.

His name is Han-shan, a kitchen helper,

the poet called Cold Mountain.

Since the day I was born, I missed his voice.

2

OFTEN I WONDER

Often I wonder, who introduced me to Cold Mountain?

Was it that tousled-haired boy in the back of my first class,

thick eyeglasses inches from poetry's page?

The bookstore owner who reached for the prescription I needed?

Or that musician-poet escaping his mill town in the woods,

a laughing monk painted in red on the case of his guitar?

Now I hand out his poems like aspirin.

"Take two," I say, "they're small."

3

HOMELESS DOGS

I languish in a car with battered friends,

the world the same as before we tried to fix it.

Young people won't listen to us, and old ones

mock our shaggy hair.

In despair, we read Han-shan's poems as we drive.

Those scribed on stones make us laugh.

Those carved on trees make us cry.

We devour these thousand-year-old biscuits

like homeless dogs!

— *after Watson #10*

4

SNATCHING SYLLABLES

My father calls to tell of my potential

with The Company. I clutch the black receiver

with my neck, keeping my hands free to write.

"Come live here and raise your family!"

blandishments any wise man would listen to.

But I am a Fool, a Trickster-King,

what good can they do with me?

Syllables buzz around my ears like flies.

I reach out with my pen and snatch them.

— *after Watson #54*

5

BUSINESS

The only job I ever heard of as a boy was business.

I could multiply, divide, solve equations, work late.

All my hands wanted to do was write, raise children, fix the planet.

No wonder I made a mess of it!

Balance sheets turned to corn stubble before my eyes.

While supposed to be adding columns, my pencil wondered

if my children, seeing me lost, would find their own way.

6

CAREERS

Why shouldn't you be an architect?

Buildings will always need authors.

Why not a civil engineer? Roads need beds.

A doctor or a priest? Bodies and souls,

like fires, will always need tending.

Why shouldn't you be a soldier?

Tyrants will always have business

with buildings and roads

and bodies and souls and priests.

7

BEACHED FISH

The train rattles past back porches of tenements,

backyards of suburbs, back forties of farmhouses,

on into the back country where no yard lights scatter the stars.

These lives are fly eggs.

They have no more memory than maggots have.

But flies lay eggs, and maggots swirl in the bellies of beached fish.

We come upon a carcass in the sand, and marvel

at the ivory dance among the ribs!

— *after Watson #29*

SMOKING A PIPE

Is it any better for me that it belonged to my grandfather,

his underslung jaw fearless in its grip?

The black cherry smoke wreathes up from the briar

no longer full of answers, but questions.

What I have yet to learn is only of consequence to me.

Who really cares if I understand or don't?

Still, I'll keep studying.

The smoke goes in one direction. The fire another.

9

MAN IN THE FEATHER SUIT

When people see the man in the feather suit,

their jaws drop with envy.

"What do you have to worry about?" they say.

"Warm in winter, cool in summer,

you float on floods, always eating well.

If you fall over, so what, no pain!"

A word to those who didn't grow up rich —

you try eating scornful feathers all day.

You try knowing your whole life is unnecessary!

— after Watson #57

10

ONE MORE BIRD SONG

I sit at the breakfast table, my chair pulled toward the sun.

The birds whistle to each other

while cedars and ferns crowd around.

Already I have swum the icy waters of the lake.

My skin is smooth.

The sun warms my chilled insides.

Soon I have business in the world. I'll go in just a minute.

One more sip of coffee. One more bird song.

— *after Watson #49*

11

HAN-SHAN IS THE CURE FOR WARTS

My job was eating me night and day, my wife

threatening to leave, taking even the stroller and the quilt.

A family of warts blossomed on my thumb so big I introduced them

to tellers and clerks. Ha ha, they'd say, making quick change.

Then I bumped into Han-shan in the bookstore, one hundred poems

so small I read them all. We moved to a new place.

My wife smiles out on sidewalks where children ride.

I work in a room so quiet I can hear my heartbeat.

My warts are gone, no marks, no scars.

12

CERTAINLY HE WILL WRITE A POEM SOME DAY

My years in the noisy world are broken up

with stolen patches when no sound stirs.

By day, a gregarious young fellow,

teaching, selling, tending to children.

By night, the cape of solitude. Silent Man!

Still as a Buddhist hermit, pencil fast as a scuttling spider.

Certainly he will write a poem some day.

What other wonders might he perform?

13

FOR YEARS AT THE CRY OF A BIRD

For years at the cry of a bird, I listened.

At the wave of a cornflower, I turned.

Near a bed of geraniums, I dozed.

At the brush of a wing, I awoke.

Today a lizard scurries near my feet, eyes me,

does seven push-ups. Ha! I can still do forty!

Will summer end before I taste

the armpit hair of that European girl?

14

THE POET JOKE

So three poets enter a bar.

The first gets drunk and raves.

The second seethes jealously in the corner booth.

The third? Ahhh, the third

rises up off the barstool

in smoke and flames,

ash floating in the air like dark feathers.

15

I READ SO MANY POEMS

I read so many poems eager not to like them.

And so many make it easy —

family anecdotes tarted up ragged right;

tightly-folded letters sent to other priests and Pharaohs.

But then I find language polished to the shine

of a dining room table waiting to welcome elegant couples.

Or a farmer's rough-sawn syllables fixing and feeding the world.

Or keening mourners at the graves of bees.

16

MAKING POEMS

I laugh when I make a poem.

I go to bed at night chuckling to myself, reading and writing.

I wake up in the morning chuckling to myself,

reading and writing.

Years later I wonder: Why no prizes, why no money?

Now I grieve for the joy I feel every day,

the ferns dripping with dew,

the basket of sunshine placed every day before us.

— *after Watson #28*

17

IN SPEECH, I EXAGGERATE

In speech, I exaggerate; in writing, underplay.

In speech, a zillion is a common number.

In writing, only reliable statistics.

For poems I gather precise information

reported from nerves in distant fingertips,

or from the sudden feeling that a voice has entered an empty room.

Reciting, I love to hear that voice

carrying its poem forward into the world.

18

MATING FOR LIFE

So little honestly said back then that did not include skin.

Too young to know what "bay-bee" meant,

old enough to glow at the sound.

We lay rib over rib, necks straining like swans,

and took flight together, wing upon wing,

toward a distant coastline totally familiar

that neither of us could imagine nor describe.

But where we both knew we would safely arrive.

19

PAYING TAXES

I empty the wastebasket and prepare to add columns.

Sold a stack of essays, one thin chapbook.

Wrote a poem recited at weddings,

another wheezed on either side of a deathbed.

I count parking receipts, over a hundred.

That many days sitting still, window at my back.

Surely I must have helped other poets. Just yesterday,

on the street, I gave a homeless man a ten.

20

AT THE VIETNAM MEMORIAL

His name ambushed me out of black granite, a college friend.

And with his death, a vow revealed carved on my heart

these thirty years: We who stayed must also pay.

They carried dead back to the chopper, we only carried water.

This is the way it is for us who did not go,

no matter how hard we fought to save those crouched in this dark wall.

There is no release from this blood vow

'til our names too are carved on polished stone.

21

THE RECYCLER

We pass each other on the street, your plastic bag

bursting with cans, my briefcase stuffed with books.

We nod, and I see your ragged beard is white like mine.

My shirt stained brown with morning coffee,

yours red with midnight wine,

I think we are the same man.

Passing by, you tell with your sharp eyes

you think it too.

22

BANANAS HALF BROWN

Once I threw away bananas half brown.

Now I find them delicious, syrupy sweet.

So too the old coats and jeans I patch

at elbow and knee: More life! More life!

I was never a slave to fashion,

nor chained to a daily job.

The cave where my ancestors began

feels warm to me now, this mansion cold.

23

A FINE SUMMER PLACE

An old wooden house is a fine summer place.

Cedar forest so still, clangs and thrums hush in the duff.

Past the turn in the road, raspberries, small and wet.

Here I befriend slugs and interpret their messages

at dawn with my daughter bent low in the grass.

Woodpeckers inspect my outstretched arms.

My bed is piled high with unread books.

— *after Watson #2*

24

AT THE WATERFRONT

Down at the waterfront, fish slip deeper into cold water.

On anchored yachts, young women lie back in the sun.

Look, that one rising from the hold is another beauty!

Her body signals for a mile with only bright wisps of rag!

My binoculars finally grow heavy.

Up on the bluff where I live, tourists huff, fat with small children.

Here the view that steals the breath is far-off islands,

radiant, dark green, lit with fish tails.

25

WHEN SOUND LEAKS FROM A CEDAR GROVE

When sound leaks from a cedar grove, better listen.

When falling moss rattles the window pane, better sit up.

The pileated woodpecker I chased all summer,

big as a hatchet, ratchets up a nearby trunk

and types out his elusive forest story right in front of me!

I lean back breathless from my desk,

forgetting for a moment the chair is broken.

Who would have thought I'd find a place so quiet

that what is longed for flies right in?

— *after Watson #39*

26

NEVER ALONE

You know the bird is there by the shudder in the honeysuckle,

its cluster of orange berries now less by one.

Yesterday a squall surprised me kayaking with the boys.

A ferry captain changed course should we founder in the chop.

Today I see the outstretched arms of pines

reaching toward us a mile across the Straits.

Vultures veer over a cloud of gulls scavenging morning dead.

Whatever we accomplish this day also will not be done alone.

27

MY SON READING HAN-SHAN

Frog squatting on a pond rock, my son

reads thousand-year-old eight-line poems.

He reads and laughs, turns the page

and reads and laughs, shoulders rolling.

Han-shan, my old friend, now his friend too!

As wind awakens the voice in pines

and sends mink scurrying toward solid shores,

he reads and laughs, teeth white as waves.

28

LAKE EFFECT

Is the cabin logbook still on the shelf?

For I long to write in it again.

A brief message of men's brief days

within the breathing rhythm of the lake.

Bound between wooden boards, as I recall,

it holds reminders of storms past, and snowflakes

drifting toward us off the lake

like tiny cities, each one different.

29

IN THE STUDIO OF THE POET

Visiting a cabinetmaker, you would expect to hear

the swoosh of bark off a peeler, the whine of saws,

steady breathing of the plane,

the sharp rap of chisels into dovetails,

wooden mallet taps to make the dovetails tight,

and choruses moaning from coarse to medium to fine,

followed by silent rubbing with oils by hand, missing only

the gathering of wood somewhere deep in the forest.

30

SO YOU THINK YOU'RE SPECIAL?

A thousand years ago, ten thousand poets in China

wore out their brushes scribbling "in the manner of Han-shan."

In America in the 50s, wandering beatniks and Buddhists.

Now here we go again, another aimless man slipping what he thinks

and feels into containers of eight lines more or less.

What possible good could come of such wretched imitation?

Honor? Joy? Memory? Stillness? Gratitude?

Pick a card, any card. Don't tell me what you find.

31

READING A BAD POET

I don't want to know about you!

You're just another failure.

So what you're obsessed with poetry,

scribbling your brains out night after moonless night.

I too sneeze and fart out loud.

When drunk, I too make ugly passes at the ladies.

A poem is a tuning fork embedded in the molten

center. It vibrates. It is not about *you*!

32

THINKING OF SEX LIKE THE CHINESE

Yum yum. And now tea, also carefully laid.

And a bed of rice, from which you arise to my mouth,

moist white grains clinging to smooth sticks.

And silk curtains admitting a breeze from your parting.

Outside, my friends and I cut and rake the hay,

arms working back and forth like cricket songs.

After, we gaze at the horizon of old mountains

and wonder how soon we will gather by the clear stream.

33

TZU-JAN

Hot and sour soup and spicy spring rolls,

Cambodian food warms my inner self.

Winter sun illuminates the grimy skylight glass,

making it glow with purpose,

keeping my outer self snug. Someday,

when I leave the city for islands and lakes,

there will I find myself

ablaze.

34

AX HANDLE

Ax handle in hand, I set out to make

an ax handle. I cut the wood to length,

then discover it is the rhythm of the bow saw I love.

When the knot in the branch reveals itself,

I so admire its toughness, pitch and whorl

I drop the plane, striking my foot.

The flare of pain and persistent redness

remind me each day of my love for you,

holy one, lazy cedar growing from bedrock.

— after Lu Chi's Preface to "Wen Fu"

35

LOSING MY CALENDAR

It's gone, that black brain in my pocket.

Now I know what I should have known before —

I'm completely lost.

I hang like a chrysalis under a leaf, nothing to do

but wait and see how I emerge, insides rearranged.

When my mourning ends for what I might have been,

I will be someone else. My wings will shine.

Nothing will know how to stop me except flowers.

36

EMPTYING DISHWASHER MIND

At dawn, I measure the coffee, careful to admire

the fragrant, oily beans. Then empty the dishwasher,

each spoon to its room next to the forks,

each plate nested on plate without clatter.

So often now my body moves without my mind,

which seems to enjoy what my body is doing.

Only then can I turn to the verses of my teacher,

Han-shan, a kitchen helper, to laugh off my pride.

37

WHAT WOULD YOU DO?

What would you do, unemployed at fifty-eight?

Seek out the hermit's cave where cold rain

mutters neither laughter nor tears,

stillness carpets rocky ground,

busy towns disappear past threshold stones,

a bit of food arrives as offerings to the shrine you tend,

and joy enters each dawn as a bird calling you to sing?

Or reenter the burning world to feed the family?

38

DOWNWARD DOG

I wake up early swimming in regret.

Why didn't I do things differently?

What a life I would have before me!

Now only bitter tears and a stack of bills I cannot pay.

The purple floor mat, flat and impassive,

registers my complaints. In the mountain

of light between my legs, upside down,

a photo of the family in happier times.

39

A GOLDEN THREAD TO FOLLOW

The caves outside my office teem with bankers,

brokers, pitchmen, clerks putting up the Christmas greens.

Commuters on the street splash fresh snow to slush.

How I once longed to be one of them!

Here, only a rush of steam through heated pipes.

Two children married, grandchildren fat with health,

nothing this minute to worry about.

Only a golden thread to follow, a golden ball to find.

— *after "Jerusalem," William Blake*

40

LIKE THAT!

This is how it ends, in a finger snap.

Not just the sun and the stars, but your life.

Your first day was 10,000 years long, the rest shorter.

Isn't it time you study how to snap your fingers,

wake up and learn to disappear?

If you don't, you'll disappear anyway. Like that!

Why not leave behind a poem, or a quilt!

41

THE MONK LOCKS HIS CELL BEHIND HIM

Going out, I lock the door.

What if someone stole my laptop!

Your lap is attached to you,

said the quilter, sewing her smile shut.

My grandchildren agree, fussing on it like a lumpy chair.

I have so far to go to leave my sharp-edged keys behind,

leave the door of my life entirely open,

leave whatever is inside orderly and forgotten.

— *for Chrissie*

42

MORTGAGES

Three of my children hold mortgages too fat

for their wallets, the fourth dropped out of school.

My wife is mad at me, about money too.

Soon enough this will be over. I already see

the dark entrance of the cave that calls me.

I hear the wind on the cloud-shrouded hillside.

There I will sing, and wonder, and die alone.

43

IF YOU NEVER GO TO SCHOOL AGAIN

If you never go to school again, it will not matter.

If you go to school again, it will not matter.

Some work is for farther fields, perhaps a cave,

or a hospital full of dying babies or trembling dogs.

Outside the window a birch tree shelters me

with a long arm like yours, covered in pale skin.

The school the birch attended is rooted

in teachings even more ancient than the Chinese.

— *for Dora*

44

PLUMES OF PAPER MILL STEAM

On a piece of lined paper the size of a Chinese poem,

I write a Chinese-sized poem.

The words sound like English because I stand where I was born,

on the shore of a Great Lake. Her forests and rivers

unroll around me in plumes of paper mill steam.

I hope to get to China before I die,

where paper was invented, poetry before that.

There my verses will turn into faces.

The people will nod with gentility and respect.

45

ATTACK BY THE "SERPENT OF DELUSION"*

I spent a year of my life in Hollywood, trying to live

through stories, making important connections.

Slowly, the flood of delusion receded, and I stand,

with nearly dry feet, at poetry's quiet brook.

Tomorrow is my last chance to return

to those swirling waters, armed with old pride.

Call the day after tomorrow and someone

will let you know which way I drowned.

Wang Wei, translated by Sam Hamill

46

READING A GREAT POET

Some poets are fragrant blossoms, strong branches,

even trees with roots deep as the crown above is wide.

But he is an orchard in full bloom,

pollen sticking to the noses of humming bees,

rain and wild wind,

fruit dropping faster than the multitudes can gather.

Even the sun is surprised, and wisps of moon cloud.

— *for Robert Bly*

47

SKULL

I drum my fingertips on my skull.
How hard it is, what dull music it makes!
Deep inside, an orchestra plays a thousand
variations on ten thousand thoughts.
In my ear bones, the shrill dark longing of cicadas.
A rush of blood to capillaries distant as China
orders my fingers, strike the drum again!

48

"BEATS YARD WORK," SHE SAID

A football sellout requires 70,000; a poetry reading, eleven.

On a warm Sunday afternoon in May, expect only the shop owner.

Tulips parade their colorful helmets along the margins of city porches.

Trillium cluster the forest floor like gossiping princesses.

Bursts of lilac the fragrance of passion soften even the rigors of the gas plant.

Anyone inside on such a day is clearly kin to the Buddha —

or lazy, drunk, or totally lost.

49

FIRST BORN

We backpacked your big body everywhere, even your red car.

How we worried about you worrying about you.

When you picked a mate, and she picked you,

the earth suddenly grew round again, and forgiving.

The caves of Cappadoccia, China and other old hermit homes

no longer seemed impossible, or even far.

In the firelight, it is you at our campsite by the lake.

It is your first face that flames.

50

DAUGHTER

A daughter is not a passing cloud, but permanent,

holding earth and sky together with her shadow.

She sleeps upstairs like mystery in a story,

blowing leaves down the stairs, then cold air, then warm.

We who at sixty should know everything, know nothing.

We become dull and disoriented by uncertain weather.

We kneel, palms together, before this blossoming altar.

51

ONE, TWO, THREE, FOUR

One, two, three, four parents, all dead.

One, two, three, four children out of the house.

Even the dog died, honorably.

Who knew such an interregnum waited in a life?

Time in the morning for birdsong.

In the evening to linger over sunset and wine.

In the dark of night, to wonder how it all happened.

In the hour before dawn, to know.

52

LYING IN BED, SICK, READING ARTHUR SZE

Emptied now of everything I've eaten, I feel the violence recede.

I lie all night in my rumpled clothes. No hunger. No thirst.

Arthur Sze's dragons fill the space between my bed and night.

His poems, like sections of tangerine, sweeten my whole mouth.

Like a Chinese emperor placed upon the throne as a boy,

I understand dimly that something big has happened.

My body relaxes into silken robes swaddling a pillow of jade.

I order another tangerine to be peeled.

53

FREE LAND

This is Indian land, fought over at the edges with poxes,

at the heart with slaughtered orchards and herds of slain ponies.

Squares of it fell to the starved sons of white men with older sons.

How hard they now work to fill towering grain elevators and banks.

My yard is a corner lot the size of a worn credit card.

I'm not complaining. The house is warm and full of books.

An old man grazing fields he loves easily ignores

the glistening brows of advancing mortgage bankers.

54

OLD MAPS: NORTH AMERICA

Old maps no longer tell us where we are,

but who we are.

Boot soles in Indian homelands.

Fear and desire over the edge.

The Great American Desert, a central emptiness.

Forts and missions clinging to water, remembered home.

Shorelines pecked by ships carrying name after name,

looking, still looking, for the golden throne.

— *for Brian Dunnigan*

55

INSECT DREAM

They wouldn't die, the insects fleeing the hinges of the dishwasher.

I struck them with a sponge, soft and wet.

Their segments stirred again and again to life.

I awoke, late for a meeting, in a household of grown children.

My wife, stirring beside me, urged me to close the window.

I do not believe in dreams. But I know there are lives

more ancient and powerful than my own

scurrying beneath this and every bed.

56

TO THE GNAT DROWNED IN MY WINE AT LUNCH

I hesitate before removing you with my longest finger,

your corpse a swollen comma. I wonder —

mostly protein, you would be good for a body,

better than the ruby sea in which you swam.

I saw you briefly alive, legs treading like useless threads,

transparent wings the purple of a priest's best robes.

Practically weightless, unable to fly or sink,

we tread and tread, unaware of other eyes upon us.

57

FULL MOON ABOVE FLOWER VALLEY ORCHARD

Alone at dusk, I pick scarred, stunted Haralson apples

whose tartness I love, even these troubled by diseases in bees.

The full moon appears over the ridge like a sad face suddenly lit.

My binoculars reveal far more scars than I have ever seen before.

Adolescent geese stream down her face, settling into corn stubble to feed.

I look away, scarred and full.

They do not know what the moon knows, what the apple knows.

58

A BROTHER'S RETURN

Empty pants on the chair.

Empty shoes beneath.

An empty shirt.

Empty hat in the closet with the empty coat.

In the breeze through the open window

one dawn in October, I hear you sigh.

My arms lift with goose bumps

before the empty, finger-streaked mirror.

59

FRIENDS

The scent of dinner penetrates the bedroom walls

where I nap and write poems.

Three different birds stuffed with sausage sizzle in the roaster.

How did my life become so fragrant that friends will cook for me?

Could it be that I cooked for them the night before?

Could it be that, when the car went off the icy road,

I strapped on snowshoes with the others to push it out?

SAUNA

Two men pour water on hot rocks,

naked conversation dripping poisons away.

My friend, a CEO, bares his doubts —

he can't at work, and at home his wife only defends him.

He listens as my sleepless nights cascade off me

toward the floor. Finally no more talk.

We slump in the heat, barely breathing.

Then burst out, red as peeled beets,

to roll and scrub in fresh snow.

61

AT SUMMER'S END

There comes a moment, though it may take years,

when you know the way your life would go if feet could lead.

Then every thought that follows flows

from steps your body knows it wants to take.

That feeling when the nestling, fledged,

wobbly at the edge, glides into blue.

Then builds a house that, caulked in all its seams,

will not let you go again 'til summer's end.

62

WIFE

At 58, she goes away to write a novel.

At what point will my character enter,

twenty-one, wearing sideburns and a crimson jacket?

No, not that novel. A much older story.

One that can only be written when alone,

mining veins of solace and revenge.

We send postcards to each other

overflowing with daily joys and sorrows.

63

A SLIGHT FEELING INSIDE

How dull my life has become!

My wife gone for a month, the children rarely call.

When they do, I'm rarely home.

I get plenty of exercise, and the work does not pile up.

The news arrives each day with no more than

the usual cruelties.

So this feeling flickering in my breast,

is it love, or peace, or shame?

64

PORTRAIT IN PEN AND INK

My daughter is a fine painter.

Were I to sit for her today,

she would capture the sadness in my eyes

at the mad aggression of our leaders;

that I forgot my whole life to work for money;

that in the dark future ahead,

I will leave behind only a few poems that last.

65

A MODERN HISTORY OF LOVE

The 1893 Columbian Exposition was all about electricity —

something new, irrepressible, everyone came.

Soon enough, factories edged cities with endless hard work.

Between World War I and World War II, euphoria and depression.

The stand-off in Korea marked now familiar ground: a cold war.

Then failure — Vietnam, Iraq, a scorched planet.

After all, my love, we never believed it had to end this way.

We were blind to history, deaf to news, hopeful as tiny sparrows.

66

LISTENING TO MY WIFE SNORE

If you don't have some longing in your life, don't read on.
A gap between who you are and who you want to be,
where you live and where you want to live,
what you do and your imagination,
some leap fallen short, called failure.
And then, miraculously, in darkness,
 a sound — rumbling, warm, peaceful, silken,
and you reach out to listen.

67

NESTING CHINESE TABLES

A family of six, each mitered at the corners,

each draped with hand-carved flowers and vines,

nested one inside the other inside the other, et cetera.

The way the crowded Chinese world once worked —

lives of ornament and precision at home,

the frontiers conquered but still dangerous,

full of wild trees, deserts, barbaric peoples.

68

READING THE POLISH POETS

My window air conditioner filters and hums.

The bottle of water in my hand is pure as fresh rain.

I know that any weekend I can travel to a lake the blue of religious feeling.

So when I read the Polish poets, I fall to my knees.

They speak of a different world,

air tinctured with sulfur, water thickened with blood.

Just think, I could have gone on living an aimless life believing

the full moon rising tonight before us grew sulfurous red all on its own.

69

IN THE BACK PEW

I sit in the back pew, alone with my thoughts.

The choir songs roll toward me over many heads.

The minister, a friend, speaks with poetry's tongue.

The old stories, and our lives of longing, make us weep.

Outside, the seasons come and go.

Shadows of birds flutter on the stained glass.

My grateful body stands and sings.

— *for Jim Gertmenian*

70

GRATITUDE TO KITTY

How few bird songs I know!

The other day I turned to quiet Kitty,

a painter of portraits without faces.

"You can hear the winter wren

near the center of the island," she said.

"And the barred owl near Soldier's Garden Trail."

I want to follow her, be her Disciple,

listen as she listens. There! And again!

71

YELLING AT BIRDS

Red Guards ordered the professor to the fields to yell at birds.

Blackbirds, I imagine, yelling back in alarm above the millet,

bouncing up again and again on waves of startling sound,

until they fall from the sky in exhaustion.

Among the ten thousand tales of man's inhumanity to man,

this one of man to man and bird — why does it seem more terrible,

that brilliant scarecrow, those fallen, hungry birds scattered

like Chinese characters inked only for homeless dogs to read?

72

THE MONK IS FORCED TO SPEAK

While making coffee, his practiced hands

put away dishes, wipe counters, empty trash.

Each sound of the dawn is a friend inside his head.

In gray light, another monk enters the kitchen.

 "Good morning," she says.

And as if that were not enough,

"Are you up often before dawn?"

73

BEFORE THE GRANDCHILDREN ARRIVE

This is a day for business, poetry, repairs.
Because tomorrow, early, the bedroom door will creak
open with the sun and the word "Grandpa" flood
in like Sergeant Pepper's Lonely Hearts Club Band
marching me up off the sheets and back into the human
mysteries of the world, like a young Lewis or Clark,
or some mad Spaniard, or the billion other grandparents
steadying the web of the world, feeling again its tremble.

74

IF YOU DON'T GO OUTDOORS TO PEE

If you don't go outdoors to pee, you'll miss

the yellow-breasted bird unusual in these cedar trees.

And upon your return to retrieve

binoculars a grandson who asks you, "Please,

open this," a pot of soapsuds,

a thousand bubbles floating free.

Then back to the cedar woods to seek

the now suspected chat, hear its feeding "tchek."

— for William, Gus, Olivia, Henno

75

FINDING A LOST PHOTO FROM THANKSGIVING DINNER

It fell to the floor among honeyed cornbread crumbs,

disappeared with the flesh of a raised turkey leg,

the gleam of numerous chardonnays,

the shouts and shadows of family now gone.

When we find it again, the baby's rusty squash handprint

slapped to her forehead twenty years ago

greets us like a glyph on desert rock or an ochre painting

in an ancient cave rubbled with lost or abandoned artifacts.

76

CLIMATE CHANGE

Winter comes to the north, wary now, a wounded predator,

toppling weakened spruce, falling through thin ice.

We raise our torches and howl all the long nights

against the Emperor burning brush on southern ranches.

But he is warring again, blind in acrid smoke, deaf to keening.

Our voices hoarse, our tears pathetic, flow like raging melt water

where polar bears drown and giant sunfish befuddle in Arctic seas.

77

MORNING STORM

...dark is God's wrath on the wings of the storm.
— old English hymn

The disturbed sky at morning stirs even my wife awake,

wrapping herself in the window's breathing curtain.

Solitary herons flock together, fleeing overhead.

A kingfisher speeds inland, chattering shrill warnings.

Cedars point wildly with their tips; birches raise their pitch.

A great storm splashes it heavy feet toward us through cornfields,

forests and lily bogs a hundred miles away —

a god so angry it will change the warming world.

78

ONE SATURDAY MORNING IN OJAI

Reading in bed, I listen to raindrops

clatter in patterns I do not understand.

Birds try to explain it to me.

Peacock, unnatural resident, shouts it out.

Flicker hoots a long laugh.

In a burst of distant sunshine outside the window,

I suddenly see China a thousand years ago,

my cloudy mountain home.

79

MAKING A NEW FRIEND

Kuan Hsiu, born 832, died 912, so the records say,

wrote his poems some years after my master, Han-shan.

Reading him this early autumn already red with bloody floundering,

I laugh with his rants against "Bad Government,"

smile at the "ghostly laughter" he hears in "great mad poets."

How foolish I once felt rising at dawn

to read what others stayed up late translating,

only for the pleasure of timeless friendship.

translations by Sam Hamill and J. P. Seaton

80

MORNING WALK

A dark-suited woman hurries, coffee held tight,

heels pecking the concrete.

A lean young man vaults into his pickup.

I walk barefoot, arms wide. No one sees me,

a cloud in gray sky. When will that happen to you?

You walk the same road, but no one sees?

When you sneeze, no "God bless you."

Already so blessed, you have disappeared.

EN LA CATHEDRAL DE SANTA DOMINGO DE OAXACA

I do not apologize for my foolish life.

I do not apologize for kneeling before an altar of gold,

for offering greetings to strangers,

swaying in smoky fields of incense,

murmuring prayers in unknown tongues,

admiring the gray braids of the Zapotec women

woven together at the tips, and the black eyes of their children.

I do not apologize for singing along.

82

THE UNREAD BOOK

Everyone has recommended it.

It will change your life, they say.

Who would not carry such a talisman

with him wherever he goes?

As I write these words, it lies beside me

on the bed, heavy and smooth and white,

as fine a companion as one could ever sleep with.

83

ART FIGHT

Her callused hands declare that she's a potter.

A painter too, she says.

"You can't lie with a picture or a pot —

words can be made to lie, so sight comes first."

I stop her there. Touch first, I say. Then sound.

Music and voices rumble through a mother's belly wall,

stirring the warm saltwater sea in which we swim.

That's beach foam beneath your broken fingernails.

84

SETTING LEAD TYPE

Every piece is heavy, every movement slow.

Care of this kind one is not accustomed to.

This letter, is it worth the trouble? That sound,

is it really a bird fluttering, or a door closing?

When every sacred choice is made, the lines

are bound with simple string, tied with a common knot.

Every step that comes after — the paper, the ink, the

bookstore browser — reveals only the lightness.

— for Scott King

85

PRACTICING FALL MIGRATION

Past spruce, cedar and birch, a gallery of flight

hangs against a wall of blue waves and whitecaps.

Cerulean, a bird I mean, and orange-cheeked Blackburnian,

plus formations of geese loud as a traffic jam with their practicing.

By 8:45, all that's left are astringent jays and nasal chickadees.

This is beginning to feel about right, sixty-one,

mind lively, body still, listening and wondering.

Then the orange monarchs arrive. First one, then a dozen. No sound.

86

OCTOBER MORNING

Clouds over Bois Blanc Island turn pink and orange at seven.

Sun steals through the kitchen window at seven-thirty

casting my shadow to the floor.

The tips of prairie roses, still hardy, turn gold at eight.

Four crows carry silver light glistening on their backs

as they strut across the lawn at nine.

It's taken twenty years sitting in this one place,

but I think I've learned to tell the time.

87

MY SON SLEEPING DOWNSTAIRS WITH HIS DOG TYRONE

You rub my back in the place only your hands know,

an old wound between my crooked shoulder bones.

Tyrone strolls with us down lanes of fragrant orange groves,

browses stems, turns back now and then in his elegant black cloak,

keeping in sight you who saved him from the pound 13 years ago.

I see myself very old, sitting on a sunlit rock near a single room.

Perhaps a hummingbird roars by. Feeling your hands, right there.

And I, like the dog at your feet, fall asleep loving this boy.

READING THE T'ANG POETS

I carry them with me in my pack or briefcase,

some typed into my computer,

poets who tell what they are feeling in short, pungent bursts.

Du Fu, how did you get so bitter; Han-shan

and Shih-te, so funny; Li Bai, so drunk on moonlight?

Every day you illuminate me, like sun outlining the grass.

Humans do not grow smarter over time,

or more clever, or more wise.

89

GLACIAL ERRATIC

In the fields of Wisconsin, rocks with no other names

fill cairns like hills where each was hauled.

Pieces of the distant north, carried here by ice,

buried by ice, moved one last time by human hands.

And still every spring surprises push up.

One of them is you, the other me.

Outliers. Annoyances. Joyously placed in a heap

around which all straight work eventually must bend.

90

THE HAMMERMILL LETTERSHOP LEAGUE

At the café table, five bearded men scribble and talk.

We are the Hammermill Lettershop League,

wondering out loud what we dare to feel and why.

We recite poems to each other with yawps of joy.

Next to us a table of women erupts in laughter!

Running for office, they plot how to take back our country.

Old men and young women laugh with the world,

they running in, we running out, faster and faster.

— *for U. S. Senator Amy Klobuchar*

91

FIVE CARTLOADS OF SCROLLS

An "educated man" was expected to know the contents of "five cartloads."
— "Wen Fu" by Lu Chi, 261-301CE*

Five cartloads? Please, Lu Chi, my heart is full

and only seven poets in residence there!

Crane, Hopkins, Coleridge, Han-shan, Bly, Oliver, Snyder.

OK, Frost and one Machado. Still, I don't study nearly enough.

But every time I open a scroll, a bird sings

somewhere, even in winter. Or a man walks by,

his fat boots violins in stiff snow. Or a butterfly

unrolls its long tongue into some delicious pot.

It is hopeless. I will never be an "educated man."

*translated by Sam Hamill

92

TRAVELS TO THE INTERIOR

The spice scent alone was worth the time and expense.

Then taste buds flattered by powdered delights,

brain buzzed by local drinks, eyes dazzled

by the landscapes and ruins of others.

The only country so far missed is my own.

The one shaped like a man, rivers and

canyons deep within. Ruins too.

And somewhere, a sacred spring.

93

THE OPEN HAND

One hand grips, the other makes a sign.*
— Gary Snyder

Scanning with binoculars the desert's ancient river cut,

I find what I am certain must be there — an open hand,

pecked light into dark rock with hammer stone.

No fist. No peace sign. No raised finger. No hex.

No thumbs up. No martial art. Holding nothing.

Saying only, I am here. At Lascaux. Rainy Lake. Ayer's Rock.

When will you open your hand to the painted desert in which you live?

*from "Tree Song" in "Left Out in the Rain"

94

CARVED BONES

The sharp bones found in an ancient cave

lured fellow humans toward its ravenous ochre mouth.

The carving of those bones hooked me on poetry,

flaking and sanding all night to get the syllables

toothed and sharp, a perfect emblem of my desire,

a beautiful curved thing thrown whistling

toward your heart to nourish mine.

95

LANDSCAPE PAINTING OF THE NORTHERN SUNG

Among mountains and rivers without end,

a cold cliff face fills most foreground space.

In distant mist, past rocks and stringy pines, one tiny traveler

pauses near a grid of groves where the trail bends upward.

Hidden beneath his cowled robes are notebooks

filled with poems, bitter and sweet, and stolen oranges.

Whichever way he goes — step forward, turn back —

mountains and rivers are the bigger story.

96

ORACLE BONES

There can be no end to their meaning.

Stories spin from them over a thousand

years like butterflies across a summer field.

Another thousand like snowcapped mountains

you have heard of but never seen.

And five thousand before that like ghosts you have seen —

teachers, friends, family, all loved, shadows

breathing under the drowsy eyelid of earth.

97

GOOD LUCK POEM

The poet rubbed up against me, wanting some of my good luck.

I loved her for that, wanted to give it to her, and the others.

These open hands that cure the headaches of strangers,

that seek a way to hold the world.

Touch these poems. Rub off some sweet bit of what they feel.

Then pass them along to a stranger.

You'll feel lighter without the clutter,

the stranger heavier with a pocketful of luck.

— for Susan Firer, Jim Hazard, Freya Manfred, Thomas R. Smith

98

WHAT AM I DOING NOW THAT I'M IN PARADISE?

What am I doing now that I'm in Paradise,

Michigan?

Writing poems.

What was I doing before, in the busy world?

Writing poems, when I wasn't too busy.

What will I do when I and my poems are dust?

Do you see the breeze riffling the cool waters of the lake?

Do you hear the moan in that white pine?

99

SCHOLARS COMPILE MY BIOGRAPHY

Variant spellings: tey, ty, te, t, ski, sky.

Late in life occasionally adopted Len-feste.

One wife, apparently feisty, four children.

Number of other descendents unknown.

Developed reasonable proficiencies in advertising,

journalism, teaching and emptying the dishwasher.

Of his 10,000 poems, nearly a hundred survive.

Of those, seven are said to be enshrined in the Halls

of the Immortals. That statistic cannot be confirmed.

100

DO YOU HAVE THE POEMS OF LEN-FESTE IN YOUR HOUSE?

Do you have the poems of Len-feste in your house?

They are better for you than Scripture reading.

Take them out and paste them on the television screen

and glance them over from time to time.

— *version of Watson #100*

James P. Lenfestey is a writer based in Minneapolis. After careers in academia, advertising and journalism as an editorial writer at the Minneapolis StarTribune, where he won several Page One awards for excellence, he has published poetry, reviews and articles, plus a book of essays, *The Urban Coyote: Howlings on Family, Community, and the Search for Peace and Quiet* (Nodin Press). His play, *Coyote Discovers America,* premiered the 25th season of the Minneapolis Children's Theatre. He has published several small poetry collections, including *Saying Grace* (Marsh River Editions), *Affection for Spiders* (Red Dragonfly Press), *The Toothed and Clever World* (TreeHouse Press), and *Han-shan Is the Cure for Warts* (Red Dragonfly Press). He is co-founder of the biennial Ojai Poetry Festival in Ojai, CA, chairs the Literary Witnesses poetry program in Minneapolis, and teaches poetry at the Grand Hotel on Mackinac Island, Michigan. He is married to writer Susan Lenfestey. They have four children and four grandchildren.

In 1974, while living in Massachusetts directing an alternative high school, he came upon the book *Cold Mountain: 100 Poems of the T'ang Poet Han-shan,* translated by Burton Watson, and it cured his warts. It also turned out to be the voice he had "missed" all his life. For the first and only time in his writing life, he began to "write back" to another author. The result thirty-three years later is this collection of poems inspired by the form and sensibility of that 1,200-year-old Chinese hermit, yet brimming with Lenfestey's own humor, wisdom, insight, and delight in language. In the fall of 2006, Lenfestey visited the 81-year-old Burton Watson in Tokyo, then paid homage to Han-shan at his hermit cave in China's T'ien-t'ai Mountains.